About The Poet

Born a month before the Spring Equinox some years ago Dean Fraser feels a connection to all of nature beauteous and green.

He is a holistic poet & storyteller and a dowsing teacher.

He enjoys being out amongst nature rather than in cities. So much for the biography. Dean prefers his energy and actions to speak for themselves.

The Poems Less Spoken

Rarities and Previously Unreleased Poetry

Dean Fraser

Contents

There is no theme to this book other than making public some poems which have for too long remained hidden, and I have to say this time I like it that way. I hope you do as well – Dean Fraser.

Introduction

As I have gone about my poetic journey there are some poems from my archive of over three hundred and fifty which for some reason or other never found themselves included in any of my previous five poetry collections. They maybe did not really sit quite well enough within the theme of one these collections. Although not in print, they have nevertheless oftentimes found their way into my live poetry sets and radio show over the years.

With The Poems Less Spoken I am finally putting that right. It has been hugely entertaining for me taking the time to re-visit my archives finding poetic tales for inclusion. Taken from a period stretching back to 2012 right through up to the year I compiled this book in 2018, I do remember writing every single one of my poems and interestingly for me, my mindset at the time. This has made the entire process compelling and fascinating, as I selected the poems to include in this book.

I cannot help but notice there are still many more poems left alone in the archives having only been seen by myself. I ask your forgiveness for keeping it that way for now as I feel these still a little too personal to share for the moment.

Maybe later... another day, another book... who knows?

For the closing section of this collection I include a short film noir story I originally wrote for the pure and absolute pleasure of doing so at the time. Having shared it in my live shows a few times, I know you will enjoy it as much as I enjoyed writing it and so it finally sees itself in print.

I feel a continuing sense of gratitude to all my readers and listeners. You allow me to do what I love the most. I promise that as long as you continue to enjoy my poetic tales I will continue to write more for you…

Dean Fraser
www.deanfrasercentral.com

Asking Questions

Asking myself the answer to the question of life resulted in me coming up with my own truth (2018).

It took a while
Well okay, a goodly few decades
Looking outwards observing life
Pondering inwardly
When the student is ready

I know the answer
Oh finally, the truth is revealed
That great unanswered mystery
A "How to" manual to life
Well, it's about… questions

Every time we think what do we do?
We ask ourselves questions
Even opting out of decisions
First requires we ask of ourselves
A question…

What to do then?
If to transcend the treadmill existence

The answer is crystal clear
Still ask ourselves questions
And make them amazing ones!

To stretch comfort zones
Be in The Zone
Raising our standards
Expectations of outcomes
Firstly, ask ourselves amazing questions

Amazing questions
More amazing answers
Unparalleled amazing life
Dare to dare ourselves the only way
The quality of questions… is all

Men of Vision

I love the ingenuity of the industrial revolution; this poem celebrates these amazing pioneers and laments the lack of romance in their 21st century colleagues' endeavours (2013)

Where have all the great engineers gone?
Brunel, Thomas Telford and George Stephenson
Men of vision creating a legacy to last
Are the best inventions all now in the past?

Making railways, ships of iron, train of steam
These men one and all followed their dream
By mathematics and physics, they planned
No CGI to help them understand

With cutting edge technology and design
Geniuses of Victorian Age, way ahead of their time
Bridges and tunnels still in use even to this day
Can we really say the same of what is built today?

They Only Want To Farm

This poem came about when I read of a farmer having to allow a fracking mega-corporation onto his land, regardless of if he wished them to be there... which in this case he certainly didn't! (2013)

It started in the eighteenth century in the Highlands of
Scotland
Lairds decreed "uneconomical tenant farmers throw them
from their land!"
And then the clearances began, buildings burning, shameful
enough to make you weep
It took some seventy years to clear them all and making way
for only sheep

1970's a new decade, economic boom, prosperity, everyone
has a car
Let's build new roads, lots of motorways, to take us wide and
far
Government policy, if a farm should be in our way, go build
anyway
Cars are more important, give farmers some money, they'll go
away

Dawning of a new century, farmers' wondering what the
future could bring
At the mercy of supermarkets pricing wars; they never could
have predicted the next thing

Drilling rigs appearing all around the land, fracking, poisoning the crops that feed
Farmers once again the victims of powerful people's greed

Three Galleries In A Day

A London visit back in 2006, although the poem was written later from my notes (2014)

Friday, five o-clock train, journey underway
An idea, tomorrow do three galleries in a day!
A schedule like that should be all planned out, I agree
Not the way I do things, rather "let's just wait and see"
Leaving my hostel at eight thirty to Southbank I venture
Thus, begins the opening gallery of my one-day adventure
Dali Universe, thrilling... I love his work and abstract mind

Melting clocks, lip shaped sofas, a hundred sketches combined
Picasso exhibition in the basement, adding to the pleasure
Two hours spent there. Now it's time for my next endeavour

Walking east along Southbank, The Tate Modern stands proud
Umpteen times I've been here, my enthusiasm still unbowed
I adore surrealists, I totally get dada, a little of the modern arts
Masterpieces made from litter or constructed from plumbing parts
Three metre canvass painted purest black, almost made me faint
What was the artist thinking "wish I had some different paint?".
A Citroen van rusting in peace and literally pieces, is it a joke?
Perhaps like some of the other art, it's only there to provoke?
A thousand paintings, sculptures and visual arts have been seen
Next gallery please! To the National Portrait Gallery I convene
Past Trafalgar Square, culture lays there awaiting
Never experienced before, excitedly anticipating

Okay I have to confess portraiture never truly quite my thing
Got to visit nonetheless, with traditional art I'll have a fling
The first few paintings I observe… stood back admiring the brushwork
Even a surrealist philistine like me can see it took a lot of work
A hundred portraits later, each one beginning to look alike

Bored stiff, wearily thinking it's just about time I took a hike
Then spying a comfy chair, coffee machine, sitting peacefully
It took a few moments, as I fell deeply asleep unbelievably...

For two hours I lay snoring, until finally I awoke
When in my ear the guard of the gallery gently spoke
"Sir we close in fifteen minutes, please leave!"
Looking at the time defied anything I could believe
In less than twenty minutes my train was going
Running along Tottenham Court Road dignity forgoing
Only just... I got there... with two minutes to spare
Of these ridiculous situations it seems I have the flair

Still as I sat there travelling back, reflecting, pondering
I loved my time in London, wandering and wondering

Again, The Moon Full

Incredibly I have written four poems on the theme of the full moon looking down on humanity, this is the second in the series of such poems and finally now finds its way into print (2013)

It was a clear night as the Moon looked down with apathy
upon the dwellers on the city
Going about their important tasks with intense intent, feeling
a sense of inner pity
Meaningful and yet oh so meaningless, trying to make sense
of it all
Fit everything into the quantum soup, existence in this urban
sprawl
Such strange ingredients to work with. Moon, what say you?
Do those lost souls floating on a cloud, make you feel blue?
Our bodies borrowed from the Universe, a billion years old...
Yet renewing every moment. What will history say when our
story is told?

Camping In The English Summer

Oddly enough we did choose to go camping again after this experience!
(2015)

Camping a must... makes the experience unforgettable
On internet campsite chosen a decision later regrettable
Basic, is the kindest way I could describe the alleged facilities
Mud and lots of it, derelict shower block, medieval utilities
Pitched our tent, make the best of it, one good meal enjoyed
Darkness falls, warm sleeping bag, our peace soon destroyed
Wildest storm torrentially blows, flapping canvass, precipitation
"Will we be okay? Tell me we'll be fine" I'm asked for confirmation
"Yeah, of course we will, we're dry and safe, all is sweet"
Diplomatically not mentioning my soaking wet feet...

Just the Model

What happens when you say yes, and then find yourself wondering why you did... I need to add that I do rhyme the name Carrie with marry twice! Fortunately, she does have a name that fits into a poem rather well and yes, we really did once have such an incredibly well-developed mutual distaste for one another's company... although we were suitably professional on the day. (2013)

"Just walk naturally down the catwalk"
How exactly? For me not exactly a cakewalk
Doing a favour for a friend taking on new meaning
How did I get involved in this? What was I dreaming?
Time to confess, what I had agreed to that fateful day
A Bridal Fayre! Yes, I know... you don't have to say
Pretending to be a groom my role for the whole evening
I saw who I was paired with, made me feel like leaving
My bride for the whole event, my partner, was fair Carrie
So fond of one other we barely talked, never mind marry

The director said "walk to the end and then you two kiss"
"What?!" This is one our friends would not want to miss
Being professional, and not wishing to spoil the event
Hand in hand we walked, the kiss we couldn't circumvent
We closed our eyes and did the deed, quite quickly
Carrie and I managing not to look too sickly

How many more dresses do they want Carrie to parade?
Oh great! Only four more times to go... my day is made

Said to the director "can I change partners, have a different "wife"?"
She looked at me in horror "our brides and grooms are together for life!"
I still have the flashbacks sometimes, waking expecting to see Carrie
Maybe the trauma from that event is why I never chose to marry?

As a footnote here I feel it only fair to add that Carrie and I did reach a different level of understanding after this event. I guess you don't look at someone in quite the same light when you have spent an entire evening sharing passionate kisses in full public view with them! Wine liberally flowed backstage. After consuming practically a bottle each, our final public kiss, after our two hours working together, lasted for at least five minutes and received gasps of surprise. And when we did eventually part lips, we got a round of applause and appreciative whistles from the audience.

A Journey Too Far

This story happened many years ago and so my teenage self takes centre-stage for this poem. The memory of the day in question remains strongly imprinted upon my mind (2015)

It seemed like a good idea, the invitation inviting
Join the club for cycling, really terribly exciting
Local newspaper said, 3rd Tuesday of the Month, come along
Share your stories, have a chat, join our happy throng

Full of fine intentions, my journey now well underway
The club my destination to arrive soon without delay
Then snowing, then sleeting, then a little more snow
Turning back never occurred, onwards we will go!

Thinking as I got there, do they not have another member?
It's so quiet, could it be because this is the 24th of December?
Knocking on the door to be greeted by deafening silence
A community centre very closed, in spite of my defiance

To ride back appears my only option now
My hands and feet so chilled, I wonder how?
No feeling in my fingers, feel they might break
As the journey home, I now begin to undertake

A little more sleet, just to help me on my way
The words I thought to myself, I wouldn't care to say
Praying I would have no reason to pull up sharp or stop
If I had to use my frozen fingers, sure I'd faint and drop

Peddling along against the wind, my racing bike crawled home
With every extreme of icy weather feeling ever more alone
'Till finally our driveway, a more welcome sight I never saw.
Three long and very painful hours it took for me to finally thaw!

If some new adventure or interest you espy
The moral of this story is clear for all to learn by
Even if seems perfection and everything in which you believe
By all means go find out more, but never on Christmas Eve…

Some People

An extremely gentle rant (2015)

Some people take themselves terribly seriously
These people are to be avoided at all costs
Apparently, they give off toxic fumes...

Some people only like the sound of their own voice
These people are too to be avoided at all costs
Apparently, their ears are malfunctioning...

Some people have their headphones so loud all can hear
These people are also to be avoided at all costs
Apparently, they always have terrible taste in music...

Some people are concerned with only how they look
These people are surely to be avoided at all costs
Apparently, their heads are quite hollow...

Mistaken Identity

Two stories, which although separated by a few years, nevertheless both saw me being mistaken for somebody else (2015)

Part One

How to react and how should I greet?
When "hello Paul" is called from across the street
Thinking they mistook me for some friend they know
Pretending I hadn't heard and on my way I go
Until the day I ventured to Morecambe town
"Hello Paul" I heard again, two guys looking at me with a frown
"Why do you not answer?" one asked loudly, quite aggressively
"Hi guys! Sorry, I was miles away" while I smiled inoffensively
Being mistaken for Paul continued for more than half a year
Exactly who Paul is or ever was never did become quite clear

Part Two

Whilst in a well-known store the name of which I shan't mention
Well, okay it was Wilkinson's, a bargain being my intention
"Hello Daddy" a small child called out, looking me in the eyes
Glancing behind to make sure she meant me, hiding my surprise

Her orange hued mother turning a bright shade of red
Smiling weakly at me, her expression full of dread
What to answer? I'm pretty sure I'd never met mum before
A quick "Sorry, not me" and escape to the first floor?
Her mum saved me from further awkwardness arisen
"You know that can't be daddy, he's locked up in prison!"

Boots 3

*My mum's mother, we called her Nan, worked on Preston outdoor market
all year round (2014)*

On the cold winters morning thermal boots are pulled on
The radio announced... ground frost and the promise of snow
later in the day
And yet she is happy...
Happy because she is doing what she loves

The market is freezing in December
Icy winds blow and there is no sunlight to warm frozen hands
It's the people you see
Fellow workers on the market pleased to see her
Customers stopping by to give her a cup of tea
Camaraderie and friendship being formed over the selling of
clothes
For years she was part of the rich tapestry that made Preston
Market special
Until illness took her away
Even her thermal boots could not help her
If you walk through Preston market one cold December
day...
Say hello...although you won't see her as you pass on your
way
It's keeping a tradition alive you see... everyone said hello to
her

Totally Fitness

I found myself in a branch of an extremely well-known fitness chain for a children's party of all things, thankfully I had my trusty notebook and pen with me (2013)

All hail to those who come to worship at the temple
The temple of the body beautiful, with a strain and tremble
Music pumping, yet not really noticed
As bodies are pumping, to be noticed
Machines activated by human power
Working up a sweat "just another hour!"

Seeking to become just a little more physically decked
Body mass index and calorie counting minutely checked
Gaining bulging muscles or loosing bulges they want to shed

Weighing scales their best friend or looked at with utter dread
I too used to worship at the temple a long time ago
I've looked at life from both sides now and for me I know
Thank, but looking at these guys I don't see any smiles
Exercise is wonderful, viewing beautiful scenery, I walk for miles

Fast-Food Now!

A poem I simply had to write! The name forming the punchline at the end has been changed to avoid a lawsuit! (2012)

Of course, he looked like a clown
And yet he was also incredibly clever
The clown being an illusion
To fool people into thinking he was harmless
This amused him
That most of the population only saw the façade
And no further
It was all part of his insidious plan
Soon everyone would know him
From Brighton Rock to Borneo...Japan to Milan.

He sat there in his ridiculous outfit
With its big shoes and the red nose
And thought over the last few years
How his genius knew no bounds
His plan working perfectly
He chuckled, for once sounding like a real clown
Thinking about how gullible the public were
How easily they fell for all the hype
The hype, with no real substance behind it
Yes, Donald McRonald had every reason to be happy

Boots 5

Boots, the series of poems I have written over a few years featuring my ancestors, is brought up to date with a little of my own story (2014)

Climbing boots are pulled on early morn
He'd been up since the first sign of dawn
Three fellow free-climbing nutcases on a mission
To climb the waterfall at Mallam their ambition
Travelling light, no need to use rope
A speedy ascent, safely, their hope

One man volunteers "I'm going to make a start"
Up the rockface he climbed, completing the first part
Then came the trickier bit, climbing up the very waterfall
His friends stood and watched; four metres high… the fall
His hand slipping on wet stone, scrabbling for a moment…
feels like forever
No rope to break his descent, backwards he fell, despite his
best endeavour
Hitting the ground with a thud, his friends rushing to assist
"Are you ok", "Talk to us". With a grin their help he dismissed
He went to sit in their van, a cup of coffee and then try again
After thirty minutes he'd finished his rest, he tried to move…
pain
Argh he thought and ahh as well, he seems he couldn't stand
or walk
Calling rather loudly to his friends "Guys, I think we need to
talk!"

They took him to get checked out, it seems he'd damaged his
spine
The shock of falling, adrenalin having made everything seem
just fine

Physiotherapy following, the art of walking now regained
"Now I'm recovering, I shall climb again!" he proclaimed
Geology interested him, so to a quarry he did venture
Keep it safe he thought, for my first new adventure
Alone he went this time, he was just going to have a wander
Long way by the footpath he found his way round yonder

To the very top of the cliff, on scree he slipped and… towards
the edge he went
Until his rock hammer he slammed in the ground, to stop his
quick descent
All his weight taken on one arm for a full hour, slowly he
found solid ground
How to get back with a dislocated shoulder and nobody else
around?
The journey was "interesting" to say the least, his shoulder
was fixed
Climbing boots are pulled on early morn, with feelings that
are mixed
He still loves the mountains, the feeling of freedom, just the
rock and him
Maybe he will climb again one day, if he can do it without
breaking a limb!

Apparently, I'm Not Scottish

A more or less true story, I wouldn't be a poet if I didn't occasionally use a little poetic license... the exact facts have been altered to protect the slightly ignorant gentleman concerned, who was forgiven long ago! (2014)

I get invited sometimes for the occasional interview
This time in Aberdeen, without much thought I flew
"We'll pick you up" they said "to take you to the studio"
Quickly my lift arrived, and he asked if I'm ready to go?
Upon my reply, hearing my accent, he stopped in his tracks

"You're not a Scottish Fraser, you're just a wee Sassenach!"
"Erm… actually my roots are Celtic French not Scots see"
"Frasier became Fraser some time ago, you understand mais oui?"
He failed to laugh. As he growled "we thought you were one of us"
"Don't think we need you in our studio, nothing for us to discuss"
Standing there open mouthed, trying to take this in my stride
Am I allowed to hit him? No, the dignified exit is better, I decide
Scotland… I love the place… I've even worn the Fraser plaid
From my brief encounter in Aberdeen at least I still got paid

Inside The Boots

Sat pondering my poetry collectively known as 'Boots'
What they mean to me and what exactly are our roots?
Do these ancestors I write about feel like a part of me?
Did these people somehow collectively define who I would
be?

In this life do we live by our own free will choice?
Is it wise to be quiet and listen to the inner voice?
The question, is our destiny truly our own to decide?
Does to follow other than destiny, cause planets to collide?
Could it be our life is planned out before we are even born?
Do we always have to smell the rose and also grip the thorn?

Does making decisions and forging ahead enthusiastically
achieve more than those who wait around there passively?
Are we the total sum of the DNA that is our inheritance?
Or is who we are based purely on our own experience?
To imagine everything before us is completely pre-ordained
What motivation to get out of bed? Life would be so pained
For what it's worth I believe our future is very ours to make
What I choose to call learning, others may see as the odd
mistake

All Part Of The Plan Blues

Are some things truly better now? (2014)

Looking around and wondering how it all happened
Once familiar buildings with character now flattened
Identikit high streets, which town is it I'm in again?
It's so easy to get confused, how to stay sane?
Got to thinking, progress happens so they say
Connected to the electronic superhighway
No need to walk and visit the private retailers
Buy it all now from faceless internet purveyors

Frank's fish and chip shop closed ten years back
International fast-food outlets moved in to fill the lack
Serving their mass produced synthetic pseudo-food
Everything designed to put us in a buying mood
Superstores killing towns and cities their main mission
Green belt being lost to retail parks, whatever opposition
Buy everything you need… your shopping, insurance, don't
be shy
Get your holidays, car, glasses, groceries… they'll even bury
you if you die
Where will it all end, change has already happened, what
more?
There's no going back, that's for sure, we already closed that
door
But these giant stores create jobs, this is what the politicians
say

Yet surely a high street full of independent shops, people
could earn their pay

Tiny little malls seem to be the way of the small shop owner
A kind of mini retail theme park, and I don't want to sound
like a downer
But they used to be on the High Street and weren't called
quaint or cute.
Although that some have been able to adapt is at least astute

They say the past is nice to visit but you wouldn't want to live
there
Just seems to me some things were once better if we dare to
compare
Do we have to follow those marketing guys dreams with such
a passion?
Can being ourselves, with our own identity instead be the
fashion?
Okay I guess it's come the time to end this little ditty
Social commentary about every town and city
If it sounded like a rant, well I suppose it can be said it is
Sharing a few thoughts with you all, as I care to reminisce

Every Day A Celebration

I wrote this for a Guy Fawkes Night poetry event back in 2013 (yes, such a thing actually happened!). I include it here because it still makes me smile (2013)

Remember, Remember… the what of November?
Was sure there was something… try to remember
Dates in a diary, reminders of significance
Sure there was something…just think perchance
Perchance to think… or was it sleep?
Or is perchancing to think altogether too deep?
Ahhh, good old computer the answers I seek
To google or not? I'll just have a peek
November is Vegan Month… hurray!
I'm writing this on Author's Day… way hay!
Does it get any better than this I hear you all say
It does! Wow! 6th November is Saxophone Day!
Yet I still think I'm missing something what can it be?
Google some more and I'm sure I'll see…

Could it be the fact that on the 7th November men are supposed to cook?
Men Cook Dinner Day… hmmm… that's one I shall accidently overlook
11th November forever special… not many days in celebration of origami!
Except even better 12th is Pizza Day, with the works except the anchovy

Just in time for 15th… Clean Your Refrigerator Day, it's official
I suppose after all that pizza it's probably beneficial

Who decides these days has clearly thought it through
To name all these days was definitely overdue
20th November is Name Your PC Day and those are the facts
I named mine Meryl… after that great woman who acts
Shopping Reminder Day is 26th November… do we need
reminding to spend?
Less than one Month to go to the fateful day… will it ever
end?
Dates to remember and some to forget
Fond memories are made, some to regret

How wonderful the 29th a day to remember to floss
Why nobody thought of that before I'm at a loss
I see from google that December is incredible
Why do people always eat sprouts, they're inedible?
But no, it's not about that, presents or religion
You'll have to think laterally just a wee bit of a smidgeon
December I cannot keep to myself, I have to tell you why
December is International Month to go Wear a Tie!

2008 Blackpool – Riverdance Comes To Town

The story of the ship (Riverdance) which found itself beached a little up the coast from central Blackpool (2013)

She was in trouble, navigating the extreme weather
She was going to end up beached, no choice whatsoever
Crashing, breaking in the waves, the end was inevitable
Brave men rescuing everyone, the scenes unforgettable
Gale force winds howling like a banshee
Tilting a crazy angle, will she be lost to sea?
Riverdance the ship, there she lay on the beach
Would they manage to float her again, with the hull breach?
As she sat there rusting in peace
They cut her up, piece by piece
That year visitors to Blackpool found a new attraction to go see
Every other venue in the town takes cash, the ship was free!
An attraction in the town that cost no money to view
To the very ethics of the place it rang untrue
To the salvage crew they told their plan
Get this ship away from here just as fast as you can
Bit by bit, over a few short months she was gone
Now paying fun the tourists can focus upon

If my rhyme does sound a trifle satirical
It's not really, I'm completely non-political
Merely an observer of life and people's motivations
That Riverdance went so quickly I offer congratulations

Egotistical Me

My earlier self, looked at from the benefit of a few decades distance (2016)

Ego often being confused with self-belief...
Self-knowing...
Self-love
There being a world of difference
Taking action for recognition

Or because one has to
In order to change...evolve
Leave behind that which no longer serves
I had my peacock years
Oh vanity thy name was Dean...

This Is Reality, Babe

Help! (2012)

Is there no escape from the horror?
No exit sign for this intrepid explorer?
Been here so long, can't remember life before
Will it go away if I close my eyes and just ignore?
No, it's still there in all too concrete reality
Glass and steel executed excessive brutality
Soulless, stark bleakness everywhere
Zombie like people, do they actually care?
Everything, the sights, the sounds totally banal
As I spend the afternoon shopping in the mall

Glasson Dock Or Twilight Zone?

A visit to this small Lancashire coastal town (or is it a village?) became weirder with every passing hour (2013)

"The short cut can save us some time" I said
If only I could have foreseen what lay ahead!
Past the farm, oh yes, we were saving time and how
The pathway narrowed, turning the corner, the killer cow!
Her and her friends marching towards us without a halt
We turned and sprinted faster than Usain Bolt
Half a mile we ran back past the farm of their destination
Farmer and his son laughing loudly at our desperation

Leaping over a gate, back on the marsh, getting our breath back
For finding these strange situations it seems we do have a knack
Walking a little further, eventually it came in sight
Pleasure yachts glistening appealingly in the light
Down the road we sallied forth with a smile
Which sadly lasted for rather less than a mile
Young gentlemen outside a pub shouting across to us
No idea what they said, we didn't stay around to discuss

A café we espied, I suggested "let's take a few moments to rest"
To be greeted by "We're closed!" I said "Surely you must jest?"
She pointed us across the bridge, to a lovely mobile café
Well ok, it was an old caravan, hey it might be great, who can say?

The teenagers queuing with us must be locals was our conclusion
Unless them wearing only socks and no shoes was just an illusion
We got served eventually and ordered coffee, taken black
Black being essential, of any other choice there was a lack

Deciding departure from this place was long overdue now
Off we set of a more direct way back to the car and how!
Walking for about an hour awe see a plane circling overhead
Suddenly five people falling in the sky, we stop and stare in dread
Will we have to administer first aid? Well, this is certainly our belief
Parachutes open and safely they descend, much to our relief
We will go back again someday, just not maybe on our own!
And see once ore if Glasson Dock truly is... The Twilight Zone

Re-Invention Is Alive Here... Bristol

This was originally going to be a far longer poem telling of all those many famous people hailing from Bristol... and then I reached a point where I believed the story I wanted tell was done and so we end with Sir Bernard
(2017)

Archibald Leach he once answered to
Leaving these shores
United States of America
Life anew
Pathway to fame and fortune

Adored
Celluloid sophistication personified
Universally Cary Grant

David Prowse
Physical perfection
Bodybuilder... British champion
Once face of road safety
In half forgotten bygone days
Achieving fame and anonymity
Seen but not heard
Darth Vader

A music degree
Piano and flute
Perfect qualifications?
Perhaps they are after all?
Engineering expertise
Intellect sits alongside irony
Walking talking contradiction
That is James May

Man of mystery
He hails from Bristol
So they say
Urbanity his canvass
Art loud and proud
For the people
Making his mark, his statement
Yet who is Banksy?

Touching base in the end
Another famous son
Pioneer
Game changing visionary
Jodrell Bank the place
Standing proud and still relevant
Perhaps now more than ever
Sir Bernard Lovell... I enjoyed playing badminton with you

The Name Is Moore

Homage to a hero of mine (2013)

A sardonic smile and a raised eyebrow
Communicating volumes somehow
Body language scaled down to one eye
Contempt, love, hello or goodbye

Talking to Myself

Pondering (2013)

As I observe, I feel I need to ask myself "Why is it that people talk without thinking first?"

I see it everywhere I venture, people creating their very own version of hell and I wonder "Why would they do that? Make their life so limited and one dimensional?"

Further pondering on the matter drew me to further observe "They ask for exactly what they don't want, all the time, why would they think that is good?"

I have to admit I believe I do know the answer to that question. The answer is quite clear. Ignorance of the truth and ignorance is very rarely bliss.

It is part of every doctrine, every religion, every philosophy, every metaphysical knowledge, quantum physics, occultism… ok, you get the idea, all the wise ones say the same… You ARE what you think… Words resonate through time and space forever.

Croatia

This one always sounds impressive when I perform it... I provide the translation below so it all makes sense (or not!) I enjoy having this one in my live set (2014)

Jagoda. Krumpir.
Dobro. Molim.
Zastava. Da.
Kikiriki. Hrvatska.
Volim Te. Ciao.
Vlak. Oko.
Grudi. Moda.

Strawberry. Potato.
Good. Please.
Flag. Yes.
Peanut. Croatia.
I love you. Hello.
Train. Eye.
Breast. Fashion.

What?

Makes perfect sense to me! Yes, really!!! (2014)

Tomorrow will be yesterday in two days...yesterday was tomorrow two days ago...the only possible reality is NOW...everything else is just past/future tense...

Are You Ready?

Philosophical poetry... and big dreams are the only kind worth going for really (2012)

Spend your life dreaming about trivia and that's what you end
up with
Make your dreams big ones...big, bold and in glorious
technicolour
Paint them across your imagination and go wild
And if the dream is possible, however remotely, there is a
good chance the way will be made available to achieve your
dream
It will happen...the choice is then yours...how much do you
want it? and how brave do you feel?
Life will change
Are you ready?

Poem in 45 Seconds...

Guess how long this one took to write? About the same amount of time it takes to apply for a credit card online (2014)

Come have our credit card
It's always easy, never hard
Buy all you want, here's two grand limit
No need to save, have it now, be with it

Until the day reality hits home
It's just another form of loan
Monthly statement shows the sums
And then the true payback comes

Bench Looking Out To Sea On The Kent Coast

The bench in question is situated at St Margaret's Bay, situated between Dover and Deal (2018)

I am here before dawn
A halo of light appears on the horizon
As the sun slowly rises
Nature's morning light show plays out before me
Crimson, purple and yellow hypnotically colour the sky
Making way for the azure blue of this summer's day

Daylight reveals highways of the sea shimmering in the heat haze
Dover to Calais ferries dart between the wake of mammoth container ships
Walkers begin to processionally pass by on their way to The Cliffs
Few pay me attention

An elderly woman with a walking stick stops
She leans on the convenient railings near me
Bidding me "good morning!"
I agree that it is indeed an extremely good morning
She seems pleased with my confirmation of her certainty
As she smiles, making her way back to her nearby home

Tranquillity on this bench
A man on a mountain bike rides past
Surprised to recognise the rider as someone I know
Today he fails to stop and pass some time with me
Too intent on his exercise

I eat my lunch
Prepared in advance
Prepared whilst most of the world still slept
Observing once more the ferries
I too have travelled their route
Today my role is observation
All life going on
I look upwards towards The Cliffs
Snakes of people walk the well-trodden paths
I have also walked their route
Today is altogether more leisurely

It is calm
The glistening sea
I have witnessed it untamed
Nature unleashed
Today gentle waves lap to shore on the little beach

Here children play
Their shouts of excitement take me back to my own
childhood
Different beach
Another coast
The same feeling pervades, nonetheless

Early evening the need for more sustenance calls me
Taking my leave from the bench for a little while
A solitary seagull takes my place as sentinel
In my absence he observes
I return within the hour
The seagull sentinel is gone
He must have found other adventures more enticing
Or perhaps the need to sustenance took him away as well
I take over his post

There on our bench
My watch now

A kayak passes by protectively close to shore
The bright red of a lifejacket keeps him safe
As he resolutely paddles against the tide
To disappear out of sight around the headland
Heading for Dover I suppose
Or maybe Folkestone

The sun begins to set behind me
As darkness slowly rises across the water
Then sudden silence..
Reaching outwards with all my senses
I see the lights of unknown ships
Mirrored by lights from distant silhouetted homes above me

One bench looking out to sea on the Kent Coast
Time-shared with a seagull
There is magic in the air this day
In this seascape
For those remaining still long enough to feel it

Sam Spode (Gumshoe)

Not quite sure why I wrote this, although I suspect it's because I wanted to read the story! I see a future movie in this one and merchandising, lots of merchandising. Well okay, maybe not, still nice to get this out into print at long last (2012)

It had to rain. In this dirty town, on these mean streets, it always had to rain. Maybe the mayor didn't pay a big enough bribe to the big guy, so it rained. The kind of rain that filled the gutters and made stepping off the sidewalk like paddling in the Hudson.

I was parked in my heap across the way from a bookstore. Well, what's a gumshoe supposed to do? I was being paid real well by a dame with dyed red hair and legs all the way to ground and she didn't mind who saw them.

"I want you to watch my husband, he runs Dirks' the bookstore on the corner of 53rd and 8th". She produced a roll of bills and threw them on my blotter. I said "Sure lady, what's the sap supposed to have done?". She looked at me like I'd crawled out from under a dirty stone "That's what I'm paying you to find out!"

I sat and watched. You'll do a lot of that in my line of work, comes with the turf, like stomach ulcers and cheap bourbon. The rain leaking in through my heaps door onto my shoulder and feet didn't make me in any better kinda mood.

Just when I was deciding this bookworm dude was gonna be a waste of my $10 an hour time, the door of the shop opened and out walked my "mark", along with the kinda blonde you usually see on movie posters and from the way they were getting along I'm thinking she wasn't his long-lost maiden aunt.

Time for the sap to pose for some real nice family photos. Now I ain't no Man Ray, but I know which way to point a camera to get evidence. I sighed to myself. Another divorce case. I took my photos and then thought about following the happy couple, then I thought again. If this guy's dumb enough to carry on in his own shop, he's gonna carry on being predictably dumb and take her to the nearest nickel and dime motel.

I saved myself the trouble of tailing them, found a phone and called Mad Manny at Fingers O'Keefe's Motel on 65th. Sure enough my sap had just booked a room and had finished checking in.
I drove over there like I had all the time in the World, real leisurely like. Parked my heap and sauntered in. Manny grunted at me through cheap cigar smoke and when I produced folding stuff he gave me his pass key.
I went up to the 3rd floor and made my gentle way along to room 39. Pressed my ear against the door and could hear gasps of pleasure coming from inside. I inserted the pass key in the door as quietly as I could, I'm sure they didn't hear it four blocks away.

Opened the door. There were books everywhere and my sap was just explaining to the dame that this was a signed first edition of the Time Machine by HG Wells and if she wanted to buy it all for herself it was gonna cost her two hundred green ones.

Just my luck, no quick easy divorce case. Some smart-ass dude selling rare books, without putting them through his books.

I walked out of the Motel with plenty of folding reasons to keep quiet. I'd tell the saps wife he ain't having no affair and he'd not have to give her his house in alimony.

Justice. It's what I do in this mean town.

Travels With My
Notebook & Pen
Dean Fraser